KNOWLEDGE, EVOLUTION, AND SOCIETY

F.A. Hayek

Knowledge, Evolution, and Society

Adam Smith Institute
1983

First published in the UK in 1983 by
ASI (Research) Limited
This edition © The Adam Smith Institute 1983

'Coping With Ignorance' was first published © in the United States in 1978 by Hillsdale College, Michigan, as *Imprimis* Volume 7, Number 7.

'The Reactionary Character of the Socialist Conception' was first published © in the United States in 1978 by the Hoover Institution at Stanford University.

'Science and Socialism' was first published © in the United States in 1978 by the American Enterprise Institute for Public Policy Research.

'Our Moral Heritage' was published © in the United States in 1983 by the Heritage Foundation.

ISBN 0-906517-31-1

Printed in Great Britain by Butler & Tanner Ltd, Frome and London.

CONTENTS

'The statesman who should attempt to direct private people in what manner they ought to employ their capitals, would not only load himself with a most unnecessary attention, but assume an authority which could safely be trusted to no council and senate whatever, and which would nowhere be so dangerous as in the hands of a man who had folly and presumption enough to fancy himself fit to exercise it.'

Adam Smith, *The Wealth of Nations*
Book IV, Chapter II.

Foreword

Dr. Eamonn Butler

This volume contains four lectures which were given by Hayek in the United States, but which are not commonly available in Britain. They illustrate some of his revolutionary new thinking: on the limits of our knowledge in economics, on the evolutionary nature of a free society, and on why socialism is an outdated mistake.

The central theme running through all these lectures is that we never consciously designed human society, nor could we. We are certainly not intelligent enough for that. Our social institutions, customs and rules have rather grown in an evolutionary way, persisting where they prove useful and fading out where they are not. The result is that society—like the physical structure of animals—has evolved to a point of much greater complexity than the human mind can understand, let alone attempt to redesign. We are ignorant of the evolutionary significance of our social rules and institutions—and therefore are signally unqualified to redesign them.

The modestly complex rules of language provide an illustration. Nobody ever set out to formulate them: they simply grew. Even a child can follow and use the rules of grammar, yet they are difficult or impossible for even the wisest adult to state. But they needed no statement, no conscious formulation, to grow and to be useful.

The market economy is very similar. Nobody ever designed the price system, yet it enables the activities of millions of dispersed individuals to be co-ordinated. The millions of rising and falling prices in the marketplace tell us at once which commodities to use for our purposes, and where we must move to cheaper substitutes. At once they summarize the available supply of a product and the level of demand for it—without us having to know its origin or its uses. Fluctuating prices continually divert goods into their most productive applications without the need for central planning.

In fact, the price mechanism enables us to utilise so much information from so many sources, and therefore to co-ordinate our various and often competing purposes, that we cannot do without it. The failure of so many of the over-vaunting attempts at central economic control show how weak is the instrument of the human mind in comparison with the co-ordinating power of market forces.

But of course, the market system has evolved, and it is a comparatively recent innovation in human history. For most of our past, says Hayek, we lived in small, hunter-gatherer bands. In such a society, where individuals know each other well, common objectives can be agreed upon and common methods decided. Goods can be shared without emnity and to mutual benefit. So long did mankind spend in this tribal state that its morality still shapes our instincts: few things give deeper pleasure than this ideal.

But only the rejection of this simple socialism enabled human numbers to expand. The move towards private property allowed goods to be traded and exchanged. This exchange economy enabled labour to be divided so that each individual specialised in particular tasks. This specialization led to greater efficiency and the production of complex goods which no individual could have made for himself. And these economic improvements permitted human numbers to increase.

The growth has indeed been rapid. Most of humanity owes its existence to the heightened efficiency made possible by the free exchange economy: and to abandon it would force most of humanity into starvation. Socialism draws upon the support of our inherited instincts, but those instincts were formed in the hunter-gatherer band and are appropriate only there. More complex economies are necessary for today's numbers. And hence it is that Hayek, in the lectures which follow, argues that the socialist conception is not only many thousands of years out of date, but is mistaken and would prove disastrous.

Friedrich Hayek: Nobel Prizewinner

Arthur Shenfield

Adapted from an article published in *Criticon*, November 1974

When Professor Hayek (as the English-speaking world, where he spent thirty-one of his most fruitful years, generally calls him) was a young man, he was uncertain whether to become an economist or a psychologist. He chose to be an economist, and as a result he received in some measure the recognition of high scholarly eminence in the form of the Nobel Prize for economics, which he long ago richly deserved—and deserved to receive without sharing it with, of all people, Gunnar Myrdal. Yet without a doubt he could have become a psychologist of equal eminence; and indeed, even though he would then have claimed to be no more than an amateur in psychology, he published in 1952 a book on the nature of sensory perception (*The Sensory Order*) which ranked with the works of psychologists of the highest professional standing.

Equally remarkable is the fact that for the greater part of the past twenty years, Hayek's main interest and main field of publication has not been economics but fundamental political theory (including, in recent years, fundamental legal theory). Thus it is that what is perhaps his greatest work (*The Constitution of Liberty*) is in the latter field, though of course there is much in it which could not have been written except by a political philosopher who was also an economist. It is a work which will rank imperishably among the classics of political philosophy. Since Hayek's perception of the nature of political society is in a direct line of descent from that of the specifically British scholars of the Enlightenment, no doubt Locke and Hume, Smith and Burke, are now looking down on him from the Heaven reserved for such men and marvelling that out of Vienna there has sprung a thinker of their own sterling stamp, while the politicians and most of the scholars of their own now distressed country have long ago strayed far from the path that they opened up. So too, no doubt, is he being viewed with admiration by Acton, who was as much a Contenintal as an Englishman, and by de Tocqueville who, though in every respect a true Frenchman, was signally different from the thinkers of the French Enlightenment, among whom Hayek finds the essential source of the leading intellectual errors of our time. It need hardly be said that it is these intellectual errors which Hayek sees as the root of the destructive totalitarian tendencies of the 20th century world.

There is a further unexpected feature of Hayek's career. To anyone who knows him personally, as well as his publications, Hayek must appear to be the very embodiment of the cloistered scholarly virtues. Calm, reflective, interested above all in ideas, and standing apart from the rough and tumble which now characterises the academic world almost as much as the worlds of politics and business, he would be the last person to be found caught up in anything that smacked of a 'movement'. Yet in the Mont Pelerin Society he founded something which may indeed become a 'movement'—a danger which has occasionally induced him to contemplate its winding up. As its President from 1947 to 1960 (when he was succeeded by the late Professor Röpke) and its Honorary President since then, he has been its inspiration and guiding light from the beginning. He has always thought of the Society, and always striven to maintain it, as a company of scholars, exchanging and developing their ideas in mutual intercourse but in no way seeking to make propaganda. His first thought, when casting about for a name for the Society, was to call it the Acton-Tocqueville Society, which indicates its intellectual inspiration. He has succeeded. The Mont Pelerin Society remains a forum for scholarly intercourse, no more and no less. Yet, since the academic world is almost everywhere in the grip of ideas hostile to those of the members of the Mont Pelerin Society, those who thus suffer intellectual discomfort have tended to seek the scholarly shelter of the Society, which now has some 350 members spread through thirty-three countries and which could have many more if it opened its doors wide to receive them. Hence the Society tends to be tugged in the direction of becoming an academic pressure group, especially as some of its members are as successful in popular economic debate as in contributing to the advancement of their science in the learned economic journals. Thus the fact that the Society has so far continued to bear Hayek's very special stamp of academic detachment is testimony to the integrity of his character.

Hayek's life and work

Hayek's career has four phases. He was born in Vienna in 1899, the son of a Professor of Botany at the University. Thus he was just old enough to glimpse the charm of the Austrian civilization which died in World War I. From 1927 to 1931 he was Director of the Austrian Institute for Economic Research and from 1929 to 1931 Lecturer in Economics at the University of Vienna, where he taught in the tradition of Menger, Wieser, Böhm-Bawerk and Mises.

In 1931 he was invited to take a Chair at the London School of Economics where he stayed until 1950, becoming in 1938 a naturalised British subject, which he still is. In England, between the World Wars, he found still alive many of the admirable features of the pre-1914 civilisation which had already departed from Austria, though obviously even in England the seeds of decay had been sown.

In 1950 he accepted an offer to take a Chair at the University of Chicago, the most celebrated centre in the United States of scholars championing the free market economy and the free society of which that economy is the shield and support. There he stayed until 1962, when he entered his fourth phase by returning to German-speaking territory. From 1962 to 1969 he held a Chair at Frieburg-i-B, the academic home of the late Professor Eucken and his neo-liberal followers, and no other place in Germany could have been more congenial to him. Retiring in 1969, he came back to his native Austria, where he now teaches as a Visiting Professor at the University of Salzburg.

Hayek's scholarly work (apart from his contribution to psychology mentioned above) falls into three main parts; first, pure economic theory; second, problems of economic policy; third, fundamental political philosophy and legal theory.

Works on economics

His earliest works in economic theory were *Monetary theory and the Trade Cycle* (published in German in 1929, in English in 1933), and *Prices and Production* (1931). In *Monetary Theory and the Trade Cycle* he applied the insights into the monetary system successfully developed in Vienna, notably by Mises, to the phenomenon of economic fluctuations; and in *Prices and Production* he sought to apply to the same phenomenon the well-known Austrian concepts of round-aboutness and variations in the period of production.

In the monetary field it is perhaps hard for us to realize how strong the grip then was in the German-speaking world of nonsensical monetary notions, without which the great German and Austrian inflations could not have happened. In the academic world the grip of these notions was exemplified by the high repute accorded such works as Georg Knapp's *State Theory of Money* and perhaps even more by the fact that Knapp was thought to be a liberal. In this, as in other fields, the economists' Vienna was an island of sense and analytical penetration in a sea of confusion.

Of these two works *Monetary Theory and the Trade Cycle* was probably the more successful; but neither was wholly successful, which is understandable when one bears in mind that they were written before the great explosion of academic disputation on the trade cycle and the problem of unemployment in the 1930s. *Prices and Production* bore the marks of compression inevitable in the lectures from which it was compiled, which made it possible for critics to drive some holes through its exposition; and of course its ideas were soon swamped by the tide of Keynesianism.

Works on economic policy

After further work rooted in Austrian concepts, but displaying modifications, Hayek published in 1941 a work which has claims to a place among the finest studies in economic theory, namely *The Pure Theory of Capital*. In penetration and comprehensiveness this was a masterpiece which, though still saluted by specialists in capital theory, has nevertheless never made the full impact that it merited. By 1941, and during the decade or two thereafter, Keynes had conquered the academic world, and little attention was paid to ideas of a different provenance.

During this period Hayek was also concerned with problems of economic policy, though of course his theoretical work also obviously had a bearing on policy. He wrote little of full-length character in the field, but his contribution as editor to *Collectivist Economic Planning* (1935) was notable. This was the work that developed Mises' pathbreaking demonstration of the problem of calculation facing every centrally planned economy, which no central planner, or theoretical economist, has ever solved. Also *Monetary Nationalism and International Stability* (1937) was a warning of the grave consequences of the breakup of the international monetary order which began in 1931.

Political philosophy

The third group of works begins with *Scientism and the Study of Society* (1942–44 in *Economica*, later published in 1952 in *The Counter-Revolution of Science*), and goes on through *The Road to Serfdom* (1944), *Individualism and Economic Disorder* (1948), *The Constitution of Liberty* (1960), *Law, Legislation, and Liberty* (three volumes, 1973, 1976 and 1979), and *The Fatal Conceit* (Volume 1, 1983).

These later works are essentially of one piece. They argue, in marvellously fair, temperate, penetrating and comprehensive manner, four basic propositions.

First, that the institutions which are the warp and woof of society arise from human action but not from human design; and hence that atttempts to design society are fatal to its goodness.

Second, that in a free society law is essentially found, not made; so that it is not normally the mere will of the rulers, be they kings or democratic majorities.

Third, that the Rule of Law not only is the first and foremost principle of the free society, but also is dependent upon the two conditions set out above.

Fourth, that the Rule of Law requires men to be treated equally, but not only does not require them to be made equal but is undermined by attempts to do so.

In this period Hayek edited and contributed to the famous essays (arising out of papers read at a Mont Pelerin Society meeting) in *Capitalism and the Historians* (1954). These essays painstakingly refuted the errors of the novelists, journalists, and biased or inferior historians who propagated the widespread belief that early capitalism ground the worker down into misery. That the belief dies hard shows how powerful a grip myth of this kind can aquire on the public mind.

Scientism and the Study of Society is a superb analysis of the errors which arise from the attempt to apply the concepts and methods of the natural sciences to the social sciences. *The Road to Serfdom* is the famous essay which warned the world that centralized economic planning would inevitably lead to the end of the liberal society which was Europe's, indeed mankind's, highest social achievement. Since it was a tract for the general reader, did not Hayek here abandon the stance of the scholar in favour of that of the propagandist, so out of character for him? The answer is *no*. If the word 'propaganda' be given the non-pejorative sense which is due as much as is the pejorative sense, the tract was indeed propaganda. Yet it is in every line a work of scholarship, as evidenced by some who did not agree with it, notably the late Professor Schumpeter.

It is true that there is a sense in which the western world, to which it was addressed, has by-passed its warnings. For it foresaw the downward slide to serfdom as the specific result of centralised economic planning, and if the West had persisted with such planning, so dear to the 'intellectuals' of Hayek's time of writing, we should almost certainly have by now reached the end of that road. Instead we have taken the road of inflation, governmental profligacy, and uncoordinated governmental intervention into the market; and this must lead us to the serfdom that Hayek foresaw just as certainly as centralised planning, if perhaps more slowly. Indeed, since uncoordinated governmental intervention can lead only to chaos, it will itself produce a clamour for true central planning, unless forestalled by the re-education of the public, and thus bring us to serfdom by Hayek's original road.

In *Law, Legislation and Liberty* and in *The Fatal Conceit*, Hayek develops two themes of revolutionary insight. First, he explains that the complex rules and customs on which our civilisation is based were never consciously planned, but arose and flourished in an evolutionary way, persisting because they worked and helped mankind to prosper. We never understood their full effects: and hence the chaos which inevitably occurs when we try to design society afresh. Second, Hayek argues that the socialist conception is many thousands of years out of date. It derives from the instincts which served us well in primitive hunting groups: helping our known friends and combining effort on common purposes. But civilisation is now dependent on quite different rules, rules which enabled us to expand beyond the primitive group. To return to an instinctive socialism would thus be to consign a large proportion of humanity to starvation.

It is principally these two insights that are illustrated in the essays which appear in this volume.

Coping with Ignorance*

It is to me not only a great honour but also the discharge of an intellectual duty and a real pleasure to be allowed to deliver a Ludwig von Mises memorial lecture. There is no single man to whom I owe more intellectually, even though he was never my teacher in the institutional sense of the word.

I came originally from the other of the two original branches of the Austrian School. While Mises had been an inspired pupil of Eugen von Böhm-Bawerk, who died comparatively early and whom I knew only as a friend of my grandfather before I knew what the word *economics* meant, I was personally a pupil of his contemporary, friend and brother-in-law, Freidrich von Wieser. I was attracted by him, I admit, because unlike most of the other members of the Austrian school, he had a good deal of sympathy with a mild Fabian socialism to which I was inclined as a young man. He in fact prided himself that his theory of marginal utility had provided the basis of progressive taxation, which then seemed to me one of the ideals of social justice.

It was he who, just retiring as I graduated, sent me with a letter of introduction to Ludwig von Mises, who as one of the directors of a new temporary government office concerned with settling certain problems arising out of the treaty of St. Germain, was looking for young lawyers with some understanding of economics and knowledge of foreign languages. I remember vividly how, after presenting to Mises my letter of introduction by Wieser, in which I was described as a promising young economist, Mises said, 'Well, I've never seen you at my lectures.'

That was almost completely true. I had looked in at one of his lectures and found that a man so conspicuously antipathetic to the kind of Fabian views which I then held was not the sort of person to whom I wanted to go. But of course things changed.

The meeting was the beginning. After a short conversation, Mises asked, 'When can you start work?' This led to a long, close collaboration. First, for five years, he was my official chief in that

*The Adam Smith Institute is grateful to Hilsdale College, Michigan, for permission to reprint this lecture, which formed part of the Ludwig von Mises lecture series.

17

government office and then vice president of an institute of business cycle research which we had created together. During these ten years he certainly had more influence on my outlook of economics than any other man.

It was essentially his second great work, *Die Gemeinwirtschaft* of 1922, which appeared in English translation only fifteen years later as *Socialism*, that completely won me over to his views. And then in his *Privatseminar*, as we called the little discussion group which met at his office, I became gradually intimately familiar with his thinking.

I do not wish however to claim to be an authoritative interpreter of Mises' views. Although I do owe him a decisive stimulus at a crucial point of my intellectual development, and continuous inspiration through a decade, I have perhaps most profited from his teaching because I was not initially his student at the university, an innocent young man who took his word for gospel, but came to him as a trained economist, trained in a parallel branch of Austrian economics from which he gradually, but never completely, won me over. Though I learned that he was usually right in his conclusions, I was not always satisfied by his arguments, and retained to the end a certain critical attitude which sometimes forced me to build different constructions, which however, to my great pleasure, usually led to the same conclusions. I am to the present moment pursuing the questions which he made me see, and that, I believe is the greatest benefit one scientist can confer on one of the next generation.

I do not know whether my making our incurable ignorance of most of the particular circumstances which determine the course of this great society the central point of the scientific approach would have Mises' approval. It is probably a development that goes somewhat beyond his views, because Mises himself was still much more a child of the rationalist age of enlightenment and of continental rather than of English liberalism, in the European sense of the word, than I am myself.

But I do flatter myself that he sympathised with my departure in this direction, which I like to describe briefly as a movement back from Voltaire to Montesquieu. It is the outcome of this development about which I am now going to speak.

Our inevitable ignorance

I've come to believe that both the aim of the market order, and therefore the object of explanation of the theory of it, is to cope with the inevitable ignorance of everybody of most of the particular facts which determine this order. By a process which men did not understand, their activities have produced an order much more extensive and comprehensive than anything they could have comprehended, but on the functioning of which we have become utterly dependent.

Even two hundred years after Adam Smith's *Wealth of Nations*, it is not yet fully understood that it is the great achievement of the market to have made possible a far-ranging division of labour, that it brings about a continuous adaptation of economic effect to millions of particular facts or events which in their totality are not known and cannot be known to anybody. A real understanding of the process which brings this about was long blocked by post-Smithian classical economics which adopted a labour or cost theory of value.

Prices versus planning

The misconception that costs determined prices prevented economists for a long time from recognizing that it was prices which operated as the indispensable signals telling producers what costs it was worth expending on the production of the various commodities and services, and not the other way around. It was not the costs they had expended which determined the prices of things produced.

It was this crucial insight which finally broke through and established itself about a hundred years ago through the so-called marginal revolution in economics.

The chief insight gained by modern economists is that the market is essentially an ordering mechanism, growing up without anybody wholly understanding it, that enables us to utilize widely dispersed information about the significance of circumstances of which we are mostly ignorant. However, the various planners (and not only the planners in the socialist camp) and dirigists have still not yet grasped this.

I do not believe that it is merely present ignorance, which we expect future advances in knowledge will remove, which makes a rational effort at central planning wholly impossible. I believe such a central utilization of necessarily widely dispersed knowledge of particular and temporary circumstances must forever remain impossible. We can have a far-ranging division of labour only by relying on the impersonal signals of prices.

That here and now we economists do not know enough to be justified to undertake such a task as the planning of the whole economic system seems to me so obvious that I find it increasingly difficult to treat the contrary belief with any respect.

It is a basic fact that we as scientists have to explain the results of the actions of men, which produces a sort of order by following signals inducing them to adapt to facts which they do not know. It creates a comparable or similar problem of coping with ignorance such as the people in economics would encounter even more than the people who undertake to explain this process.

It is a difficulty which all attempts at a theoretical explanation of the market process face, though it appears that not many economists have been clearly aware of the source of the difficulties which they encounter.

If the chief problem of economic decisions is one of coping with our inevitable ignorance, the task of a science of economics trying to explain the joint effects of hundreds of thousands of such decisions on men in many different positions has to deal with an ignorance as it were, of a second order of magnitude because the explaining economist does not even know what all the acting people know; he has to provide an explanation without knowing the determining facts, not even knowing what the individual members in the economic system know about these facts.

The theory of complex phenomena

We are in this respect not in the happy position in which the theorists of a relatively simple phenomena find themselves. When they have formed a hypothesis about how two or three variables are inter-related, they can test such a hypothesis by inserting, into their abstract formula, observed values to replace the blanks, and then see whether the conclusions are correct.

Our problem is that even if we have thought out a beautiful and possibly correct theory of the complex phenomena with which we have to deal, we can never ascertain all the concrete specific data of a particular position, simply because we do not know all that which the acting people know. But it is the joint results of those actions which we want to predict.

If the market really achieves a utilization of more information than any participant in this market process possesses, the outcome must depend on more particular facts than the scientific observer can insert into his tentative hypothesis which is intended to explain the whole process.

There are two possible ways in which economists have endeavoured at least partly to overcome this difficulty.

The first, represented by what today we call microeconomics, resignedly accepts the fact that because of this difficulty we can never achieve a *full* explanation, or an exact prediction of the particular outcome of a given situation, but must instead be content with what I have occasionally called a 'pattern prediction' or earlier, a 'prediction of the principle'. All we can achieve is to say what kinds of things will not happen and what sort of pattern the resulting situation will show, without being able to predict a particular outcome.

This kind of microeconomics attempts, by the construction of simplified models in which all the kinds of attitudes and circumstances we meet in real life are represented, to simulate the kind of movements and changes which we observe in the real world.

Such a theory can tell us what sort of changes we can expect in the real world, the general character of which our model indicates, which reduces (not so much in scale as in the number of distinct elements) the facts with which we have to deal, to make its workings still comprehensible or surveyable.

I still believe that this is the only approach which is entitled to regard itself as scientific. Being scientific involves in this connection a frank admission of how limited our powers of prediction really are. It still does lead to some falsifiable predictions, namely what sorts of events are possible in a given situation and which are not.

It is, in this sense, an empirical theory even though it consists largely, but not entirely, of propositions which are self-evident once they are stated. Indeed, I doubt whether microeconomic theory has ever discovered any new facts. Decreasing returns, decreasing marginal productivity or marginal utility, decreasing marginal rates of substitution were of course all phenomena familiar to ordinary people even if they did not call them by that name. In fact, it is only because ordinary people knew these facts, long before economists discovered their importance, that they have always been among the determinants of how the market actually functions. What the economic theorists found out was merely the relevance of these particular facts for the decisions of individuals in their interactions with other persons.

It is the obscuring of the empirical fact of people learning what others do by a process of communication of knowledge which has always made me reluctant to accept von Mises' claim of an *a priori* character of the whole of economic theory, although I agree with him that much of it consists merely in working out the logical implications of certain initial facts.

I recognize with him microeconomic theory as the only legitimate economic theory because, and in so far as, it recognises the inevitable limitation of our possible knowledge of the objective facts which determine any given situation; and we need claim no more than we are entitled to claim.

I will not deny that we find also in the microeconomic literature a good deal of indefensible pretence of a great deal more.

The misconception of 'equilibrium'

There is, of course, in the first instance, the frequent abuse of the convenient conception of 'equilibrium' towards which the market process is said to tend. I will not say that there are not forces at work which can usefully be described as *equilibrating tendencies*.

But equilibrating forces are of course at work in any stream of a liquid and must be taken into account in any attempt to analyse the flow of such a stream. Such a stream in the physical sense of the word of course will never reach a state of equilibrium. And the same is true of the economic efforts of the production and use of goods and services where every part may all the time tend toward a partial or local equilibrium, but long before that is reached the circumstances to which the local efforts adapt themselves will have changed themselves as a result of similar processes. All we can claim for the achievement of microeconomic theory is that the signals which the prices constitute will always make the individuals change their plans in the direction made necessary by factual changes of which they have no direct knowledge—not that this process will ever lead to what some economists call an equilibrium.

Not content with this limited insight, which economics can in fact supply, economists ambitious to make it more precise have often spoiled microeconomics by a tendency which we shall encounter in a more systematic form when I pass on to the second type of approach, macroeconomics. They tried to deal with our inescapable ignorance of the data required for a full explanation, the macroeconomic one, by trying measurements I shall discuss later.

The lure of false measurement

I will make only two further comments on this. The first is that it is an erroneous belief, characteristic of bad mathematicians, that mathematics is essentially quantitative and that, therefore, to build on the great achievements of the founders of mathematical economics, men like Jevons, Walras and Pareto, one has to introduce quantitative data obtained by measurements. That was certainly not the intention of the founders of mathematical economics. They understood much better than their successors that algebraic mathematical formulae are the pre-eminent method for describing abstract patterns without assuming or possessing particular information about the specific magnitudes involved. One great mathematician has indeed described a mathematician as a maker of patterns. In this sense mathematics can be very helpful to us.

The second point which I want to make is that particular reasons which in the physical sciences make measurements of concrete magnitudes the hallmark of scientific procedure, for a very definite reason do not apply to the explanation of human action. The true reason why the physical sciences must rely on measurements is that it has been recognised that things which appear alike to our senses frequently do not behave in the same manner, and that sometimes things which appear alike to us behave very differently if examined.

The physicist, to arrive at valid theories, was often compelled to substitute for the classification of different objects which our senses provide to us a different classification which was based solely on the relations of objective things toward each other.

Now this is really what measurement amounts to: a classification of objects according to the manner in which they act on other objects. But to explain human action all that is relevant is how the things appear to human beings, to acting men. This depends on whether men regard two things as the same or different kinds of things, not what they really are, unknown to them. For our purposes the results of measurements (at least so far as these are not performed by the people whose actions we want to explain) are wholly uninteresting.

The belief derived from physics that measurement is an essential foundation of all sciences is very old. There was more than 300 years ago, a German philosopher named Erhard Wiegel who strove to construct a universal science which he proposed to call Pantometria, based as the name says on measuring everything. Much of economics, and if I may add in parenthesis much of contemproary psychology, has indeed become Pantometria in a sense, by the principle that if you do not know what measurements mean, measure anyhow because that is what science does. The social sciences building at the University of Chicago indeed still bears since it was built 40 years ago on its outside an inscription taken from the famous physicist Lord Kelvin: 'When you cannot measure, your knowledge is meagre and unsatisfactory.' I will admit that that may be true, but it is certainly not scientific to insist on measurement where you don't know what your measurements mean. There are cases where measurements are not relevant. What has done much damage to microeconomics is striving for a pseudo-exactness by imitating methods of the physical sciences which have to deal with what are fundamentally much more simple phenomena. And the assumption that is is possible to ascertain all the relevant particular facts still completely dominates the alternative methods of dealing with our constitutional ignorance, which economists have tried to overcome. This, of course, is what has come to be called macroeconomics.

The errors of macroeconomics

The basic idea on which this approach proceeds is fairly simple and obvious. If we cannot know all the individual facts which determine individual action and thereby the economic process, we must start from the most comprehensive information which we can obtain about them, and that is the statistical figures about aggregates and averages.

Again, the model which is followed is provided by the physical sciences which, where they have to deal with true mass phenomena such as the movement of millions of molecules with which thermodynamics has to deal, where we admittedly know nothing about the movement of any individual molecule, the law of large numbers enables us to discover statistical regularities or probabilities which indeed, in this way, provide an adequate foundation for reliable predictions.

The trouble is, unfortunately, that in the disciplines which endeavour to explain the structure of society, we do not have to deal with true mass phenomena.

The events which we must take into account in any attempt to predict the outcome of particular social processes are never so numerous as to enable us to substitute ascertained probabilities for information about the individual events. As a distinguished thinker, the late Warren Weaver of the Rockefeller Foundation has pointed out, both in the biological and in the social sciences frequently we cannot rely on probabilities, or the law of large numbers, because unlike the positions which exist in the physical sciences, where statistical evidence of probabilities can be substituted for information on particular facts, we have to deal with what he calls organized complexity, where we cannot expect to find permanent constant relations between aggregates or averages.

Indeed, this intermediate field between the simple phenomena of the physical sciences, where everything can be explained by theoretical formulae which contain no more than two or three unknowns, and the instances where a large enough number of events to be able to deal with true mass phenomena to rely on probability, is our subject. In the social sciences we have to deal with phenomena which are not made up of sufficiently large numbers of similar events to enable us to ascertain the probabilities for their occurrence.

In order to provide a full explanation we would have to have information about every single event which you can never possibly obtain. But while micro-theorists have resigned themselves to the consequent limitations of our powers and admit that we must be content with what I have called mere pattern predictions, many of the more ambitious and impatient students of these problems refuse to recognise these limitations to our possible knowledge, and possible power of prediction, and therefore also of our possible power of control.

What drives people to the pursuit of statistical research is usually the hope of discovering in this way new facts of general and not merely historical importance. But this hope is inevitably disappointed. I certainly do not wish to underrate the importance of historical information about the particular situation. I doubt, however, whether the observation and measurement of true mass phenomena has significantly improved our understanding of the market process. What we find by this procedure, as by all observation of particular circumstances, may possibly be special relations, determined by the particular circumstances of the moment and the place, which indeed, perhaps for some time may enable us to make correct predictions. But with general laws which help to explain how, at different places, the course of economic affairs is determined, these quantitative relations between measurable magnitudes have precious little to do. Indeed, even the very moderate hopes which I myself had at one time, concerning the usefulness of such economic forecasts based on observed statistical regularities, have mostly been disappointed. The concrete course of the process of adaptation to unknown circumstances cannot be predicted. All we can predict is certain abstract features of the process, not its concrete manifestations.

It is now frequently assumed that at least the theory of money, in the nature of that subject, must be macrotheory. I can see no reason whatever for this. The cause for this belief is apparently the fact that the value of money is usually conceived as corresponding to an average of prices. But that is no more true than it is of the value of any other commodity. I do not see for instance, that our habitual use of index numbers of prices, although undoubtedly very convenient for many purposes, has in any way assisted our understanding of the effect of monetary changes, or to draw relevant conclusions, except, perhaps about the behaviour of index numbers.

The interesting problems are those of the effect of monetary changes on particular prices, and about these index numbers or changes of general price levels, tell us nothing.

Conclusion

It seems to me more and more that the immense efforts which during the great popularity of macroeconomics over the last thirty or forty years have been devoted to it, were largely misspent, and that if we want to be useful in the future we shall have to be content to improve and spread the admittedly limited insights which macroeconomics conveys.

I believe it is only microeconomics which enables us to understand the crucial functions of the market process: that it enables us to make effective use of information about thousands of facts of which nobody can have full knowledge.

Science and Socialism*

Some time ago, it occurred to me that the moment had arrived in which it would be worthwhile to organize a great public discussion on the question *Was socialism a mistake?*. I gained the support of twelve fellow members of the Mont Pèlerin Society to act as a team in the affirmative, and our plan was to challenge a similar team from the other side to a public discussion, which we hoped to hold in Paris.

This proved to be impractical for two reasons that are also interesting. One is that an affair like this, on the scale on which I had contemplated, is very expensive, and our efforts to raise funds from the capitalists was a failure. Evidently, the capitalists did not have an interest in the intellectual defence of capitalism. In fact, the largest offer I got was from the leading man in German banking, who, on my request for an amount of 400,000 German marks, presented me with 3,000 German marks. But that was not the main point. I think if we had persisted, we might even have succeeded in raising funds on a more lavish scale.

A much more serious consideration arose when we assembled at the Mont Pèlerin meeting in Hong Kong. It was then suggested that if we selected the opposite team, it would have no credibility. There is a great deal of truth in this. The upshot of this discussion was that I was asked to write out the challenge in book form, submit it to the twelve members on our side, elaborate it, with help of their criticism, into a small book, and make the book the challenge, by inviting the other side to organise its own team for the public discussion.

Now, sitting down and writing this out, I found that merely explaining, as I had done as basis for a debate in somewhat theoretical terms, the reasons why I believed that socialism could not possibly work and that the whole scheme was a mistake, would not be adequate. This caused me to undertake the writing of the second, much longer, part of the volume, which I intend to call *A Disquisition on the Reactionary Character of the Socialist Conception*.

*The Adam Smith Institute is grateful to the American Enterprise Institute for permission to reprint this talk.

Scientific or value questions?

This is the topic that I want to discuss, and I will give you an outline of the ideas that I think are of some importance. One has to face a certain issue that economists have been wary of facing—the argument that this is all a question of value judgments and therefore cannot be scientifically decided. I am convinced this is mistaken because, posed as a question whether a given aim can be achieved at all, this also involves the question whether the values and moral and ethical principles which guide us are reconcilable with each other and with what we really want. These are eminently scientific questions.

I have arrived at the conviction that the neglect by economists to discuss seriously what is really the crucial problem of our time is due to a certain timidity about soiling their hands by going from purely scientific questions into value questions. This is a belief deliberately maintained by the other side because if they admitted that the issue is a scientific question, they would have to admit that their science is antiquated and that, in academic circles, it occupies the position of astrology and is not one that still has any justification for serious consideration in scientific discussion. It seems to me that socialists today can preserve their position in academic economics merely by the pretence that the differences are entirely moral questions about which science cannot decide. This issue leads into an intellectual and I believe strictly scientific analysis of the interaction of our changing moral beliefs and the economic and social structure of society.

The evolution of morality

The starting point is a very simple one. There can be no doubt that our innate moral emotions and instincts were acquired in the hundreds of thousand years—probably half a million years—in which Homo Sapiens lived in small hunting and gathering groups and developed a physiological constitution which governed his innate instincts. These instincts are still very strong in us. Yet civilisation developed by our gradually learning cultural rules which were transmitted by teaching and which served largely to restrain and suppress some of those natural instincts. Although we are still inclined to describe these as 'good instincts', we must, to a large extent, suppress them in order to maintain our type of society and an economic order upon which that society can depend.

There is, in this sense, a conflict among different moral rules, but a conflict with which we can deal scientifically because the question is: Would people who are really aware of these conflicts still opt for the satisfaction of their moral emotions? Or would they not have to admit that those rules of conduct, which culture has gradually evolved, which we have not designed, which we have not chosen because we knew that they are good, but which in fact have enabled us to develop a system of worldwide division of labour and exchange, are now the essential condition for achieving what practically everybody wants—even those people who are nostalgic for primitive forms of society.

In a short talk like this, I must put the argument in a slightly pointed form; I cannot give all of the fascinating details which appear if one pursues these issues, but I will point out two crucial points. For the small hunting and gathering band, consisting of twenty-five to fifty people, there were two overriding moral conceptions which today we describe with the terms 'solidarity' and 'altruism'. Solidarity means common purposes pursued together with our fellows. We all know the elation which we experience in the present day when we find ourselves joining in the pursuit of common purposes with our friends. William James's famous 'moral equivalent of war' is a good illustration of this characteristic feeling. Yet, there can be no doubt that while in the small group it is a necessity that all the members spontaneously pursue the same ends in a commonly known situation, obedience to this instinct would have prevented any expansion of society.

The expansion of society was due to the fact that individual members did not have to obey compulsory common concrete purposes, but were free to pursue ends that might differ from those of fellow members of the group.

The same applies to the second traditional 'good instinct', which still governs our emotions, but which had to cease to be obligatory to make the great society possible: the principle of 'altruism'. This is a little more difficult to discuss because the concept itself is so ambiguous and obscure. But there are one or two things which can briefly be made clear: altruism can extend only to the known needs of known other people; it cannot lead to the growth of a society which depends on our serving the needs of people of whose very existence we have no idea.

The duty of altruism is one of choosing between the magnitude of known needs of known other people and the urgency of our own needs. But when it comes to serving the needs of people of whose very existence we do not know, altruism cannot guide us. Altruism, in the sense that we must serve the needs of our known neighbour before we pursue the profit from dealing with strangers, would have made impossible the extension of society beyond the small group.

It is these two instincts, deeply imbedded in our purely instinctive or intuitive reactions, which remained the great obstacle to the development of the modern economy.

If I had time to think I could write the whole of economic history in terms of the gradual subduing of these good natural instincts by culturally developed rules of conduct which no longer concerned concrete ends and concrete needs of known people, but were purely abstract rules of behaviour having little to do with what our instincts told us to do.

The conflict of old and new morality

Ever since this drastic change there has been in us a continuous conflict between two conceptions of morals: the learned morals or rules of conduct which we have gradually acquired, and which different parts of the population have accepted to different degrees, and the deeply ingrained, emotional, natural, and, as we still call them, good instincts. It is no longer instinct, nor reason, but learned traditional rules of conduct which mainly govern our lives.

I think the first member of the small group who exchanged something with an outsider, the first man who pursued his own ends, not approved and decided by the head, or by the common emotions of the group, the first man above all who claimed private property for himself, particularly private property in land, the first man who, instead of giving his surplus product to his neighbours, traded elsewhere—not to speak about the later development with money and money lending, particularly money lending with interest—contributed to the development of an ethics that made the worldwide exchange society possible. This had to be achieved, however, in constant struggle with the predominant opinion of the group in which he lived—opinions supported by the wise old men—and, once there was a state or authority or organized religion, both by the state and by religion.

I need not give you further instances; the most common illustration is, of course, the gradual acceptance of usury against the whole Christian teaching on the subject.

There can be no doubt that, say, the Athenian producer of ceramics could always have found some other poor Athenian who would have gained from having another jug or, at least if this producer of jugs had instead given more attention to his oil trees, from a jug filled with oil. In fact, this jug filled with oil went to the Black Sea and brought the grain by which the majority of the Athenian citizens could live. Although the motive for the action was purely selfish, the effect of the action was eminently beneficial to the support of the poor of this society.

All the trading centres of the world, around the Mediterranean and elsewhere, gradually developed through such no doubt countertribal actions by which the individual pursued his own interests, but ultimately produced in this manner supplies which made it possible to feed a larger population of his town.

All of this developed, of course, in a competition among groups, each imitating those who adopted a somewhat advanced—from our present standpoint—system of practices and, in consequence, increased more rapidly in population, both by procreation and by attracting people from the other groups.

I suggested before that the whole of economic history could be rewritten in terms of this gradual suppression of the primitive instincts by what we very mistakenly call 'artificial' rules. Of course, they are not in the strict sense artificial. Nobody ever invented them. They were not the result of design. The new manners of conduct were not adopted because anybody thought they were better. They were adopted because somebody who acted on them profited from it and his group gained from it, and so these rules, without anybody understanding them—that is very important for the later part of my argument—without anybody understanding in what way they benefited their community, gradually came to be generally accepted.

If I had time to elaborate on this connection between the change of our moral rules and economic development and opportunities for more and more people to survive in a gradually expanding and finally worldwide economy, I would have to elaborate on the history of the hero of that development who, in current books of history, is usually still represented as a monster—the moneylender. I think it

32

was largely the moneylender, and his gradual acceptance as a tolerated and even respected person, who made possible the development of what we call capitalism. And yet the history of morals and opinion still tends to treat the moneylender, or even the ordinary trader, as a kind of parasite; and in most parts of the Orient he is still a member of the lowest of classes.

You will find that economic evolution was made possible by a constant change of recognised morals and by a gradual proliferation of rules of law, which had already in classical antiquity led to the formulation of an essentially individualist, private law, with the recognition of private property and contract. This commercial spirit was temporarily—I'm afraid I agree here, to some extent, with Gibbon—destroyed under the influence of Christianity and again revived in modern times. By the eighteenth or early nineteenth centuries, these new morals, which I will call the 'commercial' morals, had, in the Western industrial world, spread almost universally. What may at first sound surprising is that even a hundred years ago, more people took these morals of the market as a matter of course than do so today. But this can be easily explained. As long as small enterprise predominated, whether it was the small farm or the small tradesman, not only the head of the enterprise, but every member, assistant, or child learned what might be called the rules of trade in his daily activities.

I think as long as there prevailed a world of small enterprise, these commercial morals were, in the Western world, universally accepted, except perhaps by the church, but the church made a very ineffective protest against it. So far as economic life was concerned, I think its teaching had lost practically all influence.

The cause of present problems

Then, in the course of the past century, two fundamental changes occurred which are the cause of all of our present-day problems. One was the rise of the large organisation, whether it be big enterprise or government, whose members no longer learned automatically these rules of trade. The first generation might still have learned from their parents to respect the traditional rules of the market; the second generation, the children of employees who, themselves, often entered salaried status in a business organization or became civil servants, no longer learned from childhood up. As a matter of course, the practices of finding customers, of competing with other sellers, of having to find an occupation, were recognised moral practices.

The conception of the responsible head of a family whose duty it was to build up capital, both for his family and for his business, has ceased to dominate general opinion; these traditions ceased to be in the flesh and blood of every member of society. People came increasingly to regard them as inherited conceptions of which they had heard, but which had no meaning for them. This social change deprived society of a moral view which had already become traditional, of automatic acceptance—a moral tradition which had succeeded merely because it had worked, but which nobody could justify and for which nobody—I am afraid, not even the economists—really could provide an adequate justification. This moral system on which the formation of a worldwide market rested increasingly lacked credence and was partly destroyed, with the assistance of a new philosophy. In the seventeenth century, Hobbes, and particularly Descartes, at first in the intellectual, and then in the moral, field stated that one must not believe anything which cannot be proved. This view gradually spread, especially in the eighteenth century, and in the nineteenth century this philosophical doubt about traditional morals suddenly became practically effective. The loss of the moral beliefs which had been essential for the maintenance of the existing market system was suddenly given a sort of intellectual foundation. It came to be believed that the ruling moral beliefs were unfounded, were pretences contrary to instinct and reason, and were invented for the protection of those who would profit by them. The young decided that since nobody could explain why they should obey these morals rather than others, they were going to make their own morals. Only morals which had been deliberately designed for a recognised common good purpose could really be accepted as worthy of a fully adult human race. And the purpose would have to be the satisfaction of the innate natural instincts of man.

All of this is familiar; I don't think I have to give detailed evidence. But in a rough outline, this was the history of the late nineteenth and early twentieth centuries in which what I have called the 'moral foundations of an exchange economy' were demolished. The reformers often explicitly appealed to these primitive feelings which the conventional morals had suppressed.

Just look at the role the conception of solidarity plays in the history of socialism; look at the number of times which, to the present day, the appeal to altruism occurs in the socialist argument. Of course, this preaching fell on very fertile ground. It fell on the ears of people in whom the instincts which they had inherited were still very much alive and only repressed by the now discredited learned morals.

This is the state in which we find ourselves now, and I fear we have arrived at a point when what an English statesman said ninety years ago—that we are all socialists now—applies today to the great majority even of the anti-socialists. They all have the feeling that, of course, these basic fundamental moral truths, like the desirability of solidarity, the desirability of altruism, ought to apply to our economic activities. That might be a very beautiful world, but today it is no longer possible. Yet people like John Stuart Mill dreamed that, though we are not yet quite ready for socialism, some day it is bound to come, because it will be the triumph of these basic ethical instincts which, since they are in all of us, we cannot permanently suppress.

We must admit that the replacement of the concrete goals that we pursue by the observation of purely abstract signals has been not only the sole possible way in which a worldwide division of labour could have been created, but also the only way in which today we are able to maintain an economic order which, by making use of much more information than any one person possesses, can keep the present population of the world alive.

The shortcomings of modern economics

I fear modern economics has not really done its job in this respect by making it clear to the public that the price system is the indispensable condition, not only of our wealth, but of the survival of a large part of the population of the world. A system of market-determined prices is essentially a system which is indispensable in order to make us adapt our activities to events and circumstances of which we cannot know. Where economists have become so misleading—I am here returning to the subject of an essay of forty years ago on *Economics and Knowledge* in which I started on these reflections—is in describing beautifully how a given system of data determines the particular organisation of society, suggesting that all we have to know are these 'data' in order to bring about by deliberate organisation a much better utilisation of resources than is actually achieved.

They were wrong in two respects: one is that at least the mainstream of economics, neoclassical economics, never clearly brought out what I call the 'guide' or 'signal function' of prices. That was due to the survival of the simple causal explanation of values and prices, assuming that values and prices were determined by what had been done before rather than as a signal of what people ought to do. We can only fit certain phenomena into our scientific concept of the structure of the world if we give up the aim of explaining events by a single cause. We have now learned that frequently the behaviour of the individual is determined by his success in maintaining himself as part of a certain system within which it is not a single cause but the whole system to which he has adapted that determines his behaviour. For this reason, value cannot be explained by a single cause, but can only be understood as the determinant of what people must do to maintain the overall structure.

The second point is that economics proceeded on the assumption of 'given data' and produced a beautiful, aesthetically satisfying theory to show how these data determined the resulting order, but one forgot that these data were purely fictitious; the data were not given to anybody. They were in that sense fictitious because the economists merely succeeded in demonstrating that if they knew all the facts, they could determine the results. But, in fact, the market process operates not because we, or others, know all these facts, but because the mechanism we have built utilises the knowledge of facts dispersed among millions of people by means of the signals which teach us how to adapt to events of which we know nothing, to the changes in supply of resources of which we have no direct information, and to changes in demand and needs of which we also have no direct knowledge.

I am afraid I have become—with all aesthetic admiration for the achievement—more and more sceptical of the instructive value of the construction by which at one time I was greatly fascinated, that beautiful system of equations with which we can show in imagination what would happen if all these data were given to us. But we often forget that these data are purely fictitious, are not available to any single mind, and, therefore, do not really lead to an explanation of the process we observe.

36

The task

I believe our task—a task which in my opinion must end in the purely intellectual refutation of all socialist conceptions—is to show how only a market and a competition-determined price system can enable us from day to day to adjust a worldwide division of labour to ever-changing circumstances and to maintain that degree of productivity which we need in order to keep the population of the world alive and to continue the growth we have made possible by adopting this system. I believe we can now demonstrate, and ought to say so publicly, that socialism is altogether based on an intellectual failure to comprehend the conditions under which we are able to produce enough to satisfy our expectations. And that will be, in a more elaborate form, my justification for proposing an affirmative answer to the challenge I am going to issue on the question, *Was socialism a mistake?*.

The Reactionary Character of the Socialist Conception*

Our innate instincts and emotions have been shaped by something like a million years in which the human race lived in small bands of thirty to fifty people in a hunting and gathering life in which all their emotional attitudes, still embodied in our physical constitution, were gradually developed. Our instincts tell us, first, that our duty is to serve the visible needs of our known friends; and, second, that the activity that gives us most satisfaction is to join in a common effort for common ends.

These feelings are very deeply ingrained in our constitution. In a way, we all still feel like that. But we have to recognize that the development of civilization was based on our gradually learning new rules of conduct that involved restraining and taming those primordial instincts. Civilization has grown by our learning rules that taught us to restrain and suppress what we still call our natural instincts and to learn entirely new practices, superimposed on our natural instincts, and restraining them, which built modern civilisation.

I could talk about this subject, which has long been one of my main interests, for a great length of time. I will merely give two illustrations of what are still our natural instincts, which we had to restrain and suppress in order to build a modern civilisation. The first is our wish to serve the known needs of our known neighbours. The second is to join with our fellows in the pursuit of common purposes. These are the basis of the small society and what, in a million years of existence in small groups, became a part of our physiological make-up.

The new morality

Rules on which the growth of civilisation is based are very largely rules that told us we could disregard these primitive instincts. By following instead certain abstract rules of conduct we could do more

*The Adam Smith Institute is grateful to the Hoover Institution at Stanford University for permission to reprint this address.

good—not by aiming at the satisfaction of the needs of known people, but by following the abstract guides of market prices that led to the formation of modern society. There is no question that the international economy arose because people disregarded what were the dominating rules. The first traders in the Mediterranean who, instead of giving what they had to their known neighbours, travelled overseas to exchange it for something else that they brought home, certainly severely infringed on the traditional codes.

Instead of seeking the elation that we still all feel when following common purposes with our known fellows, the first people who decided to pursue their own ends, which their fellows did not share, were certainly infringers of traditional rules. But it was this gradual evolution of rules that were contrary to man's natural instincts that enabled us to build a worldwide society based on exchange, in which each of us does more good by serving the abstract symbols of the market than he could have done by devoting his energy to the needs of his known and familiar fellows.

I believe you still will be shocked by my stating this so bluntly and clearly because we are still guided instinctively by those inherited 'natural' emotions. But I think we must recognize that we have become a worldwide, peaceful, and prosperous society by having learned to disregard those natural instincts and to follow instead certain abstract rules of honesty—rules establishing private property and ultimately codified in the form of private law. It is the rules of property and contract on which the growth of a worldwide, peaceful, and prosperous society was based. All these are traditional rules that evolved by a process of selection, which made those groups who followed the new rules more prosperous than other groups, and which thus came gradually to govern the civilised part of the world. Those communities who adopted the new rules and, in doing so, infringed upon deeply embedded natural feelings became the successful ones, the ones who multiplied because they were more prosperous and were able to attract people from other groups. Gradually, these new traditions of abstract rules that people had to learn—rules that served to tell them to suppress some of their natural instincts—became the basis of a civilization embracing the Western world. They were rules, which for two or three thousand years, were learned by every person who took part in the exchange economy. Until one hundred years ago, every human being in Western society had to learn this market economy, based on small enterprise, on the small artisan, the small merchant, and the individual farmer, in order to succeed. The function of these rules was not *understood*; nobody really understood what depended on them. In fact, all the moral prophets fought against these new rules, but they did prevail; they did lead to the formation of an extensive and ultimately nearly worldwide society based on specialization and the obedience to formal rules of conduct that allowed every person, as long as he obeyed these formal rules of conduct, to pursue his own ends on the basis of his own knowledge.

The beginnings of doubt

Until 150 years ago no one seriously doubted these rules in the Western world, whose prosperity, whose peace, and whose freedom rested on these traditional rules of individual conduct. But then, within the last 100 or perhaps 150 years, a great change occurred. This change came from the convergence of two entirely different developments. An ever-increasing number of people, instead of learning these rules by being either masters of a small enterprise or members of that master's family or his immediate servants and thus immediately taking part in the market process, became instead members of large organizations—on the one hand, large organizations of business or, on the other hand, large organisations of government. In either activity, the new generations had no opportunity to learn from childhood the rules of the market. They learned instead the rules of the organisation; and these organisations had, in a great measure, to appeal to their primitive instincts. It was again a question of deliberately collaborating with one's known fellows for a common purpose, and the same people who no longer had an opportunity to learn to obey the rules of the market were taught that the way to success was to operate within a small group joining for a common purpose. So it was really within the last century or so that an increasing number of people grew up who no longer regarded as obvious those rules of the market society that until then had been the recognised condition of personal success and prosperity, as the unquestioned conditions of social life, but rather felt them as a strange outside imposition with which they had nothing to do. But that wasn't all. I think the effect was that more and more people no longer accepted this set of traditional rules as the unquestioned foundation of honest action because a new philosophical movement taught them that, after all, these traditional rules were nonsense. A philosophy deriving from Cartesian rationalism taught them that they ought not to accept anything that they did not understand. Now, of course, all the rules on which market society rested were rules whose importance and significance *nobody* understood. They were just traditional rules that everyone accepted. Once nobody learned them from childhood—or a very decreasing number of people did learn them from childhood—more and more people regarded them as irrelevant to their activity within their known environment. Nothing could be more welcome than the teaching of the rationalist philosophers that one ought not to believe anything the function of which he did not understand.

So the curious development occurred that it was a rationalist philosophy that made people doubt or made them reluctant to accept a discipline of rules whose significance they did not understand. It made people believe that a society that has just grown up, which was regulated by rules whose importance and significance nobody could explain, was really nonsensical and morally contemptible and that we ought to replace this tradition—which nobody really understood or knew had created our modern society—by a better, deliberately designed system of rules that would appeal to those traditional instincts that are innate in all of us.

The fatal conceit

In a sense, we all are socialists. We are still governed by feelings that are based on what was necessary in the small group of known people among whom each had to aim at fulfilling the needs of persons he knew; where he had to collaborate with a definite group of fellows, who were given to him and whom he could not choose, to pursue common purposes. Our instincts still tell us to strive to serve the known needs of known people and that our pleasure in life is derived from the consciousness that we follow a set of common purposes with people whom we know and who share our environment. This, of course, is a fact that has often been noticed. We all know James's famous phrase about the moral equivalent of a war—that what people want is an awareness of the pursuit of known common purposes, that that is what gives them satisfaction; and we cannot be surprised that a great mass of people were captivated by the new doctrine, that instead of following the traditional rules of conduct that had made a great impersonal abstract society possible, they ought to return to a society that better gratified a natural instinct to serve the known needs of known people. It is a rather curious fact that in this movement, two completely different traditions converged: an appeal to innate, primitive instincts, and the ultra-rational argument of the latest philosophers—that one ought not to respect anything that one could not rationally justify. The Cartesian doctrine that one ought not to believe anything to be true that could not be demonstrated to be true was applied to the moral rules that one ought not to obey any rules of conduct that were not recognisable as serving known common purposes.

The foundations of modern society

Our whole modern society, based on a far-ranging division of labour, is, however, essentially dependent on two factors that conflict with our natural instincts. The first is the assumption, implicit but not understood, that we can do more good to unknown people if we follow the impersonal signals of the market, which enable us to serve the needs of people whom we do not know and to make use of opportunities and facilities with which we have no direct acquaintance. The second is that for this purpose we can follow our own individual aims with freely chosen associates and are not bound to serve the concrete ends of the group into which we were born.

The obedience to purely abstract rules of conduct that leads to the formation of a social order was the result of people accepting a tradition whose significance they did not understand. But then they were told that all this is nonsense; that they ought not to accept these superstitions but recognise that only in a deliberately organised society will they knowingly do good; that they ought to aim at known benefits to known people, and only this will secure them the gratification of their natural instincts. Closely connected with this is the feeling that one ought not to work for one's individual aims but will feel the supreme elation that a person can experience only if he joins with his known fellows in the pursuit of some known, common purpose. I think we all know that it is more pleasant to know that one works for the needs of one's immediate familiar environment or for a common purpose with our known fellows rather than pursue alone one's individual ends, that is, to pursue one's own profit irrespective of what one's immediate neighbours do.

42

It was thus two practices on which our material advance was based and that the conventional moral code justified: the pursuit of profit rather than the satisfaction of known needs and the emancipation from the compulsion of sharing the common purposes of the small group into which we were born. We did build an international economic order that increased human productivity infinitely. We must admit that we are now in a position to maintain even the very lives, not to speak of the prosperity, of the enormously increased population of the world, only because we no longer aim in our personal effort at the satisfaction of the known needs of known people, but because we are wholly guided by the signals of the market that lead us to serve the needs of people whom we do not know and enable us to make use of the facilities provided by other people of whom we know equally little. In a sense, it is rather surprising that all people in the world are not socialists. Because in the present state of general knowledge, unless one really understands what mechanism makes possible our prosperity or even our capacity for keeping alive the present population of the world, I say that it is surprising that not all people are contemptuous of the traditional abstract rules of the market and long for a return to a system in which they know that they are serving the needs of known people and can join in the common efforts of their fellows. That, indeed, is our present position. Emotionally, ninety-nine per cent of the population of the world are socialists; but if they had their way, they would destroy the spontaneous order of the market and thereby the mechanism to which we owe the capacity of keeping alive the present population of the world. At the present moment and for the immediate future, I see very little hope of persuading large numbers of people that by obeying the rules of the market, by relying on the purely formal rules of law without any central direction, we can achieve more than if we were to return to a system in which we are all working for known purposes in concord with our immediate fellows aiming at the same concrete ends.

In fact, so long as the present predominant views continue to govern public opinion and governmental policies, I believe the hope of preserving that order, to which we owe not only our prosperity but also our capacity to maintain the population of the world, is very small. I am in the habit of saying that if the politicians of the new, present world do not destroy this world during the next twenty years, there may be hope for the gradual emergence of better understanding. And I am confirmed in this by the experience that while, when I was very young, only the old people still believed in a free system, and while I was in my middle age, nobody except myself and a handful of others believed in the principles of classical liberalism, there is now hope because a new generation begins again to discover the rationale of the system that had prevailed in the past without being understood, but which it is beginning to understand and preach. Our hope for the future, the hope of the preservation of civilisation, must rest not merely on leading scholars recognizing the true connections, which they are still very far from recognizing, but on our succeeding in persuading those makers of opinion—whom I call the intellectuals, these secondhand dealers of ideas—who understand that our capacity to maintain not only our present level of wealth, but to maintain the present population of the world, depends on our relying on the spontaneous order of society.

Our Moral Heritage*

What I am going to discuss is the problem of how what I call the extended order of human co-operation ever arose. I used to call it the 'extended society', a term which is somewhat similar to the descriptions the 'Open Society', or the 'Great Society'. But I have come to the conclusion that the term 'society' itself is a misleading expression, an attempt to persuade us that this great order of our activities is due to our instincts towards our immediate fellows. The term 'society' is really a misnomer, because in contrast to what our instincts tell us to do, what I call the extended order of human action is due to our gradually learning to submit to what I can only describe as *restraints* on our instincts.

The extended order of human co-operation is due to restraints on natural instincts

Because they are acquired, we very much dislike, and even hate these restraints. There is a great conflict between, on the one hand, the innate instincts which we acquired living in the small hunter-gatherer group where everybody knew the same things, shared the same ends, and knew the same limited group of people; and on the other hand, the new kinds of attitudes which we never deliberately chose and never understood, but which enabled us to form an order far extending the range of our sensory perceptions.

I sometimes like to say—and I think this is more significant than a mere simile usually is—that our learning a traditional morality, which largely involved restraining our inherited instincts, is a step in evolution as important as the addition of the sense of vision to the sense of touch. There was one time when animal organisms were possessed only of a sense of touch, and were, of consequence, aware only of what happened in their immediate neighbourhood. And then, perhaps a hundred million years ago, they acquired the sense of vision and became aware of what happened at a distance.

Now, we too have acquired a further sense, what psychologists would now call an extrasomatic sense, not built onto our physiology, but allowing us to adapt ourselves to events which happen far

*The Institute is grateful to the Heritage Foundation for permission to reprint this lecture.

beyond our vision. We are living in a society which exists only because we are capable of serving people whom we do not know, and even of whose existence we are ignorant; and we in turn constantly live on the services of other people of whom we know nothing.

Adam Smith was the first to perceive this state of affairs, that we have found a method of creating an order of human cooperation which far exceeds the limits of our knowledge. We are led to do things by circumstances of which we are largely unaware. We do not know the needs which we satisfy, nor do we know the sources of the things which we get. We stand in an enormous framework into which we fit ourselves by obeying certain rules of conduct that we have never made and never understood, but which have their reason. It was those groups who happened to fall on these rules of conduct prospered and multiplied, while other groups, who tried other things, failed.

Morality is not the product of intelligence

In this I have been led, by a very painful process, gradually to reject what in my youth I regarded as the latest insight, and what even my great master, Ludwig von Mises, made the basis of his philosophy: the utilitarian explanation of ethics.

Most of us have been brought up with the conception that man was intelligent enough to discover what habits of action were more effective than others, and that because he understood how he served his needs best, he gradually accepted such institutions as private property, the family, and honesty.

All rules are of course restraints on that instinctive behaviour which is innate in us, which we acquired when we lived for many millennia in small groups, but which helped us to achieve common ends and served the needs of known familiar fellows. Gradually there evolved from this a different kind of moral tradition: the rules of property and the family, which are in essence restraints on our natural instincts.

It was the misleading belief of most of the last generation, and even most of the classical economists, that man, by his supreme intelligence, *understood* that it was better to adopt these different rules. But that is not true. Man never understood why he accepted these morals. The morals of property and the family were spread, and came to dominate a large part of the world, because those groups who by accident accepted them prospered and multiplied more than others.

We do not owe our morals to our intelligence: we owe them to the fact that some groups uncomprehendingly accepted certain rules of conduct—the rules of private property, of honesty, and of the family—that enabled the groups practising them to prosper, multiply, and gradually to displace the others. Man was never intelligent enough to design his own society, but the practices that helped him to multiply his numbers, spread for just that reason. It was a process of cultural selection, analogous to the process of biological selection, which made those groups and their practices prevail.

But the fact that our morals are not the result of man's supreme intelligence discovering that they were better, but were the result of a process of cultural selection, explains why we all so much dislike them.

In an essay some two years ago, I remarked that man was civilized much against his wishes. I think that this is fundamentally true. for the fact that these rules were not founded on an understanding of how they operated, but merely prevailed because those groups which adopted them were in fact more successful than others, caused us to be torn constantly between two attitudes. On the one hand are the kind of emotions which were appropriate to our behaviour in the small groups where we lived together for over a hundred thousand years, where we learned to serve our known fellows, and where the whole group pursued the same aims. On the other is the more recent development in which we no longer chiefly serve known fellows, where we no longer pursue common ends, but where we have found the mechanism to keep alive in this world, roughly speaking, about two hundred times as many human beings than there existed before civilisation began.

I think that it is roughly true that ninety-nine and a half per cent of the people now living in this world are enabled to live by the development of new forms of human interaction which men in the small group did not know, whose function we do not understand to the present day, and which they only very reluctantly obey and follow.

The principles of property and the family are evolutionary successes

The process by which the ethics of private property and honesty came to prevail and why the groups which obeyed these rules increased and multiplied more rapidly than others, is one interesting problem with which I must briefly deal. For how could a tradition, whose effect people did not realize, prevail and be passed on from generation to generation, if people had no rational understanding of it?

The answer is that all human groups could exist only by obeying some kind of rules of conduct which they had in common. But to preserve rules of conduct whose functions they did not understand, they drew upon the aid of supernatural sanctions. And we must admit that we owe it to mystical beliefs, that we preserved a tradition which was beneficial to us. Thus we owe our civilisation to beliefs which are not true in the same sence in which scientific facts are true, but which are just as essential because it is due to our belief in them that we have been able to develop our modern civilization.

It is a very interesting fact that, among the founders of religions over the last two thousand years, there have been many who were against property and the family: in fact, I believe that you will find about every ten years some new creator of a religion that is against property and the family. *But the only religions that have survived are those which support property and the family*. If you look at the present world, you will find that, with the exception of communism, all the world-wide religions (whether the monotheistic creeds of the West, or the exotic religions of the East) support the two principles of private property and the family. Even though thousands of religious founders have reacted against this and have advocated religious beliefs opposed to these two institutions, their religions have not lasted very long. 'Not very long', in this sense, means not more than roughly a hundred years.

I think that we are presently watching one such experiment already in the state of decline before its hundred years are over. Communism, is, of course, one of these religions which are anti-property, and anti-religion, which had its time, and which is now declining rapidly. We are watching one instance where the process of the natural selection of religious beliefs disposes of yet another mistaken one, and restores the basic beliefs in property and the family.

Why the institution of property was so beneficial

I must still explain why I believe that the belief in the institution of private property—or, as I prefer to call it, several property, because it is not necessarily the property of individuals but the properties of any group—is an essential condition of the development of the extended order of human co-operation.

The transition from the human relationships of the small groups based on common ends and common knowledge, to the society which utilizes widely dispersed knowledge, and serves a wide variety of different individual purposes, has enabled mankind to make use of an infinitely greater amount of information than any small society ever could.

Private property, of course, was never 'invented' in the sense that people foresaw what its benefits would be. Its main benefit turned out to be the division of labour which it brought about. That in turn increased the possibility of maintaining a larger number of people because it generated an increase in productivity by enabling us to utilize a much greater variety of information than could ever be possessed by any single agent.

But even more than that, it meant that an increase in population did not become, as Malthus predicted, a process where the increase of humanity led to decreasing returns, and therefore to a decrease of personal incomes. On the contrary, it was found that insofar as it made possible an increase of human numbers that was due to increasing differentiation, the increase of population was *not* subject to the law of decreasing returns. In fact, the increase of the density of population increasingly helped to *improve* productivity.

Malthus's application of the law of decreasing returns to increasing humanity, was based on the assumption that human labour is uniform. But the great development made possible by property was that human labour and human capacities became highly specialized.

And so the increase of population became an increase of variety. It made possible the institution of what Adam Smith was the first to recognize as the division of labour. Smith taught (but his successors did not understand) that the division of labour was a direct function of the extent of the market. And the extent of the market, of course, is a consequence of the increase of population. The increase of the population, far from reducing productivity, and far from leading to impoverishment, is in fact the source of the increase of our productivity, and the increase of our capacity to keep alive ever-increasing numbers of men.

The self-regulating nature of population increase

I am at the point where, I confess, I have come somewhat into conflict with the belief of most of my contemporaries among the economists, and even more with popular opinion. We have all been taught that the greatest danger to mankind is the rapid increase of human numbers and that there will soon be 'standing room only'.

But I maintain (and I am very glad to have found suppport in the work of one or two recent economists such as Julian Simon, who have made this a special study) that this is all wrong. It is not true that the increase of population leads to impoverishment. There has been no instance in history—and I say this after careful consideration—that increases of population have led to impoverishment of the people who were already there.

The contrary impression is due to the fact that we are speaking about *average* incomes, and not of the incomes of the people who are *already there*. But the evolution of the division of labour, and of capitalism, has favoured the poor more than the rich: it has led to a greater increase of the number of the poor than of the rich. The result is that an increase of population generally leads to a decrease of *average* incomes, simply because the poor multiply more rapidly than the wealthy, and the wealthy more rapidly than the very rich.

Now, this does not mean that the people who were already there become any poorer, only that more poor people are being added. In a sense, it turns out (although in a meaning quite different from that which Karl Marx intended) that the contention that capitalism created a proletariat, is perfectly true. It gave them life. They could never have existed if the capitalist system had not made it possible for the propertyless to survive, whereas in an earlier system they could not survive. That is nothing to complain of. Our morals, the morals which have prevailed, the morals of private property and honesty, are simply those which favour the practices that assist the multiplication of mankind.

The economic calculus is a calculus of life: it guides us to do the sort of things that secure the most rapid increase in mankind. In a sense, I am prepared to defend this contention by saying that life has no other purpose than itself, by which I mean that we have been so adjusted that our actions contribute to produce more human beings than there existed before. But I do not think that there is any reason to be horrified by this. Of course, we have to admit that evolution has not been guided by aesthetic ends, and I admit that I am not very pleased when I visualize the fact that economic prosperity in the foreseeable time is likely to lead to a very rapid further increase of mankind. Yet I believe that the fear that this will lead to the horrifying state of 'standing room only', is entirely misleading.

It is an interesting fact of economic advance by way of the market economy that the greatest proliferation of man occurs only at what one might call the periphery. In the highly advanced countries (what we used to call the 'capitalist', or 'market' economy countries), people no longer use their greater wealth to produce larger families. That happens only on the periphery, on those parts of the world which have joined the West, but did not originate with the West. The best illustration are the admittedly depressing shantytowns surrounding all the rapidly-growing cities in the world, whether it is Mexico or any other great city in Latin America or the Far East.

Most people are horrified by seeing such life that 'capitalism' produces. But these are not people who have yet fully taken over the morals of capitalism. Although they have joined the leading capitalist centres, they still strive to satisfy that instinct which they have inherited from the primitive small society: to produce enough children to ensure that enough survive to support them when they are old.

I think that I could demonstrate, if I had the time, that this multiplication of mankind, which so alarms most of us, is due to a very peculiar situation in which we find ourselves.

I have used the term 'periphery' of the market economy, the margin of people that have joined the communities which have a fully developed market economy. I believe that this periphery has now reached the maximum extent it can reach: the border between the advanced capitalist countries and the underdeveloped countries has reached its maximum. And since the effect of the efficiency of capitalism is very largely on the margin, we live at the time of the maximum rate of multiplication of mankind. As more and more regions and territories are fully absorbed into the market economy, this margin or periphery, which has now reached its maximum, must of course shrink.

So we are living in period of the most rapid multiplication of mankind, observing the traditional rules which were selected because they were most beneficial to the multiplication of mankind, does not lead to an indefinite multiplication. It is a process which is self-regulating. As the advance order of society expands the part of the world where people have learned to control their numbers, the periphery of people who profit from it and are thus enabled still to satisfy their primitive instinct of providing many children, will become smaller.

Socialism removes the self-regulating mechanism

I think that this present fear of the effect of the morals of the market economy in producing an indefinite increase of the number of mankind is mistaken. It is a test of our success that we are able to maintain larger numbers wherever we wish to do it: but only where we *wish* to do it. It is not an inevitable process.

I must also add that there is one exception to this principle. I claimed before that I know of no instance in history when an increase of population led to the impoverishment of the people already existing, but I must add one exception. That is when governments redistribute incomes, and thus subsidize the development of people who cannot maintain themselves. The increase of population is a danger *only* where redistribution of incomes by government subsidizes the increase of people who will never be able to maintain themselves.

There are certain consequences which follow from this for our policy with regard to the underdeveloped world. I will give only one very brief illustration.

There are parts of the world where it is quite clear that climatic and other conditions will never enable a large population to subsist. The most famous instance is the southern part of the Sahara, where we subsidize an increase of population, people who will never be able, from all we can know, to maintain themselves. I mention this only as an instance of the harm we may be doing in assisting the expansion of populations in parts of the world which are not likely ever to maintain a larger population than they presently do. We are preparing future misery, because we must not imagine that the Western world would be indefinitely willing to maintain, in other parts of the world, populations that are larger than the conditions there are likely to support.

52

There are, thus, very serious consequences of my argument for our policy toward the underdeveloped countries. But let me return, in conclusion, to the problems of the Western world.

Traditional morality is vital to human survival

The conclusion of what I said is that we owe not only our prosperity, but our capacity to maintain a population as large as that to which the Western world has grown, to obeying certain traditional rules or morals, essentially the rules of property and the family, whose functions we have never understood, which people dislike because they do not understand their function, and against which the great revolutionary movements of our time, socialism and communism, are directed.

What I am trying to do in *The Fatal Conceit* is to show that their argument is wholly based on factual mistakes. They assume that it is in our power, by redistributing incomes, to put everyone on the level we would wish them to be. Now, the difference between the socialist and me is not a difference of values. Socialists like to pretend, in order to escape serious discussion, that these are questions of value judgment, and so cannot be discussed scientifically. They are, however, wrong about fact. Socialism assumes that we can deliberately reorganize the utilization of resources, so as to produce even more, or at least as much, so that the distribution of the product is more equal and more just than it is.

I am profoundly convinced that socialism is not an invention of the working class, but purely an affair of the intellectuals. But you might be shocked when I say that the writer chiefly responsible for converting the intellectuals of the Western world to socialism is a man who is regarded as the great representative of the Libertarian philosophy, John Stuart Mill. And I will illustrate with a passage in his famous *Principles of Political Economy*, originally published in 1848, and, for a hundred years, the standard textbook of economics.

Mill begins his exposition with the theory of production, and then in the second volume changes to the theory of distribution. In the first page of this volume, the following sentiment occurs: 'once the social product is there, men, individually or socially, can do with it whatever they please'.

Now, if that were true, it would certainly be our moral duty to see that this product was distributed justly. Yet if we tried to do so, the product would never be there again! The distribution of market rewards is the mechanism by which individuals are told what to do in order to make their maximum contribution to the total product. And if we try to redistribute the product for the purpose of making the distribution 'just', the mechanism no longer guides us to do what we must do in order to produce a product of the present size.

The whole idea that we can replace the market by central planning is based on intellectual error—an intellectual error, which I am afraid is very widespread, and which is shared as much by businessmen as by intellectuals. It is rare to find an exception. But I have just come across a recent public statement by a military commander of all people, and which pleases me enormously: 'planning is the replacement of accident by error'. But he was a Swiss officer, and they appear to be rather different from servants of governments elsewhere.

QUESTIONS AND DISCUSSION

QUESTION: I think that your comments on the *specific* activities of a person like Mother Theresa would give more insight than from your general theory. Specifically, she lives by a principle that 'God calls us to faith, not to success'. Do you find her activities morally and economically sound?

PROFESSOR HAYEK: Faith has helped to preserve a hundred different kinds of beliefs, since all it does is enable a group to stick to their own set of beliefs. Which of these beliefs will survive and spread depends on their economic efffect.

After all, our morality is itself the result of a process of cultural selection. Those things survive which enable the species to multiply. And those practices and habits which enable us to multiply came to prevail and became the cause of mankind increasing to two hundred times the numbers which it had before the development of civilization began.

(In fact, we have now reached the stage where, contrary to the naïve Aristotelian view of science, we realize that all order that we find in the world is the result of processes of selective evolution. Some physicists have very recently, and convincingly, argued that even the atom is the result of an evolutionary process to establish combinations of elemental particles that were resistant to destruction, surviving other combinations. There is no question that the human organism is the result of a process of selection. And the human society is part of the same process, selecting those societies which have adopted practices which are most conducive to their survival and expression.)

The great problem for social policy is that we hate the idea that we owe all our success, not to our intelligence having chosen our culture as the right thing, but to having been selected, as it were, for doing the right thing without actually knowing why it was better.

All revolutionary response against the market society is based on the idea that we want a society which serves our natural instincts. But what we call the natural instincts are precisely the instincts which we adopted during our experience in a small bands of a few dozen people, a society where everybody knew his fellow members, where everybody served the same purpose.

The morality which makes the extended order possible, has not been invented by us, and has never been understood by us; and therefore we hate it. And the people who pretend that we could return to follow our natural instinct, have great appeal. But I fear that ninety-nine per cent of the people now living owe their existence to the development of civilization. If we really adopt or follow the urge to return to the cultivation of our natural instincts, we would, in the course of a few generations, effectively kill ninety-nine and a half per cent of the people now living.

QUESTION: Professor Hayek, your remarks on evolutionary theory have reminded me of the 1960s observation of an Oxford philosopher that political philosophy in the tradition from Plato and Aristotle to Marx and Mill had petered out although 'an occasional magnificent dinosaur stalks onto the scene such as Hayek's *Constitution of Liberty*, seemingly impervious to the effects of natural selection.'

You have shown that political philosophy is indeed alive and well. However, I am not clear exactly what you're saying in your remarks; and the same questions could be asked of the *Constitution of Liberty*. Are you trying to justify a particular moral code, or are you trying to give us a mere explanatory account of ethics?

PROFESSOR HAYEK: Allow me first to refer to the quotation you cited, a comment on my work that I most resent. I particularly resent it because there is no better method of harming the development of young people than by telling them that a particular book is not one they ought to read.

But on the main topic, I am afraid that I would have to elaborate my lecture at great length to answer your point. My argument contains much of which is offensive to man's pride.

We are so proud of having created civilization thanks to our intelligence. And once you take this for granted, it is natural to conclude that if this experiment was not very successful, our intelligence should enable us to create a better world. Now that is wholly based on the 'fatal conceit' that the order of the society which we have is the result of our intelligent design. And my present aim is just to un-deceive man of this pride, which, if it were justified, of course would justify his attempts completely to reconstruct his society.

However, it was not man's intelligence which created society, but cultural evolution which created man's intelligence. Our brain does not manufacture intelligence; our brain is merely an apparatus for absorbing and learning a traditional way of thinking, a tradition both of interpretations of the world, and of rules of conduct which we have learned to follow. Thus the social order depends on a system of views and opinions which we imbibe, inherit, and learn from a tradition that we cannot modify.

I mention this only to suggest how basic are some of the differences which distinguish my present philosophy from that which is predominant in our generation. I rather expect you to revolt against most of what I have said. I only hope that you will very seriously reflect upon it.

QUESTION: Professor Hayek, you made a very optimistic statement with respect to the impending failure of communism. What is the basis of your optimism that communism is failing?

PROFESSOR HAYEK: I would not dare to make any predictions of what is going to happen in Russia, which has now a very effective military dictatorship. But I will confess that my remark was inspired by one particular experience, not very long ago.

I think it was last May, that in my London club I happened to sit on the same table as a Russian scientist, who had come to Western Europe for the first time to attend a scientific conference. He spoke quite good English, so I could ask him what surprised him most on visiting Western Europe. His answer was: 'You still have so many Marxists. We haven't any!'

THE ADAM SMITH INSTITUTE